H. Clay Glover

Diseases of the dog

H. Clay Glover

Diseases of the dog

ISBN/EAN: 9783337814755

Printed in Europe, USA, Canada, Australia, Japan

Cover: Foto ©ninafisch / pixelio.de

More available books at **www.hansebooks.com**

OF

THE DOG

—BY—

H. CLAY GLOVER, D.V.S.

SPECIALIST IN CANINE DISEASES.

inarian to the Westminster Kennel Club, New Jersey Kennel Club, Hartford Kennel Club,
Rhode Island Kennel Club, Syracuse Kennel Club, American Fox Terrier Club, Etc.

1203 BROADWAY, Cor. 33d Street, N. Y.

FEBRUARY, 1889.

DISTEMPER.

The term distemper, whose literal meaning is a deranged condition of the animal economy, is particularly applied to animals of the brute creation. To the dog, when afflicted with that disease somewhat resembling typhus fever in the human race. As canine pathology has been given more attention in the past few years than formerly, we have now become quite familiar with the nature of the disease and the remedies indicated; consequently the loss by death is comparatively small when proper treatment and attention are employed. Microscopic analysis of the blood during distemper shows the existence of bacilli life. In early days, those dogs that were fortunate enough to survive this disease, did so merely through strength of constitution and not from the assistance of any remedial agents, as utter ignorance of the subject then prevailed. The disease doubtless then appeared in a much milder form than that with which our present highly bred animals are afflicted.

Owing to more or less inbreeding that has been indulged in to intensify certain form and characteristics in dogs of most all breeds, constitution has to some extent been sacrificed. Animals bred in this way, are in consequence, less able to resist or combat disease than those with less pretentious claims to family distinction.

Causes.—Bad sanitary conditions, crowded or poorly drained kennels, exposure to dampness, insufficient or over feeding, improper diet, lack of fresh air and exercise, all conduce to the development of distemper. It is contagious, infectious, and will frequently appear spontaneously without any apparent cause, in certain localities assuming an epidemic form. Age is no exemption from distemper, though it more frequently attacks young animals than adults. Very few dogs pass through life without having it at some period. Many people are of the belief that their dogs have contracted distemper while being exhibited at bench shows. This may be the case in some few instances, but when the veterinary surgeon in charge is efficient and attentive to the discharge of his duties, there is little fear of contagion. Distemper following the exhibition of young dogs, particularly when sent from a distance, is due to their contracting cold in transportation either to or from a show, the disease following as a natural consequence, though the strain on their nervous systems may help towards its development.

Any dog having attained the age of one year, if in vigorous health, is then attacked with distemper, I know of no reason why he should not recover, providing the proper methods are employed, though occasionally a case in which numerous complications occur, such as inflammation of the bowels, fits, chorea, paralysis, jaundice and pneumonia, or broncho-pneumonia that will resist all the science of the veterinary profession. As a matter of economy, I would suggest to dog owners, especially those intending having them field broken, to subject their puppies at the age of one year, if in robust health to the contagion of distempered animals, with the object of their taking the disease, expecting them to recover. If they come through all right they may then be broken. To have a dog die of distemper after having expended from $100 to $200 on his education is, to say the least, very unsatisfactory. Again, a dog's sense of smell is sometimes so seriously impaired by the disease as to render him ever after useless in the field.

Symptoms.—In early stages, dullness, loss of appetite, sneezing, chills, fever, undue moisture of the nose, congestion of the eyes, nausea, a gagging cough accompanied by the act of vomiting, though rarely anything is voided, if anything. it will be a little mucus. Thirst, a desire to lie in a warm place, and rapid emaciation.

This is quickly followed by a muco purulent discharge from the eyes and nose, later, perhaps ulceration of either eyes or eye-lids. Labored respiration, constipation or obstinate diarrhœa, usually the latter, which frequently runs into inflammation of the bowels. There is inflammation of the mucous membrane of the entire alimentary canal, and all the organs in time becoming more or less involved. A pustulous eruption on the skin is by some authors considered a favorable symptom, but to me it is evidence of a vitiated condition of the blood. In some cases many of the above symptoms will be absent, the bowels being the first parts attacked. The following which sometimes, but not necessarily occurring with distemper, I classify as complications, viz.: Fits, Chorea, Paralysis, Pneumonia or Broncho-Pneumonia, Jaundice, and Inflammation of the Bowels, and will require treatment independent of any one remedy that may be given.

Distemper Fits differ from ordinary epilepsy inasmuch as the animal does not rush about violently, but will lie prostrate upon one side, champing the jaws and frothing slightly from the mouth, the duration of which is indefinite—perhaps lasting for hours. This I consider the worst feature in distemper. In ordinary epilepsy, the attack usually subsides in from 10 to 20 minutes. The latter will be more thoroughly·

entered into later on under the heading of Fits.

Chorea makes itself apparent by a constant twitching of the muscles. It may be local or general. Usually yields to treatment if taken at the start, but when of long standing, it is almost useless to attempt doing anything for it. I have known bitches so afflicted, to recover on being bred, the trouble disappearing entirely.

Paralysis in distemper is usually only partial, affecting the spine and hind quarters, causing loss of power, inability to rise, etc. It will first be observed by an uncertain wavering gait behind.

In Pneumonia the respiration is quick and oppressed, the abdominal muscles being employed in the act. An occasional cough, not violent, a frothy expectoration either white or of a rusty color. If the ear is placed against the right side over the region of the lungs a crackling sound or crepitation may be detected. In Broncho-Pneumonia the mucus rattle will be observed.

Jaundice will be marked by the following symptoms, viz., uneasiness while sleeping, loss of appetite, thirst. The fœces dark and thin at first, later on dry and grayish in color; colic pains. Membranes of the eyes and mouth, also the urine of a deep yellow shade.

Inflammation of the Bowels is indicated by extreme thirst, tenderness of the abdomen, colic pains, mucus and bloody discharges from the bowels.

Treatment.—The animal should be placed in warm, dry quarters, and hygienic conditions strictly observed. There should be sufficient ventilation without draughts.

With puppies I would advise at the start giving Glover's Vermifuge, as nearly all have worms, which add greatly to the irritation of stomach present in distemper. The bedding should be changed daily and the apartment disinfected two or three times a week. For this purpose I would recommend Platt's Chlorides, as I consider it the best disinfectant made, being a combination of chlorides put together on scientific principles. It is perfectly odorless and not like the many so-called disinfectants, which are merely strong odors overpowering less strong ones.

Feed frequently on easily digested, nutritious diet, such as beef-tea or mutton broth, thickened with rice. Let all food be slightly cool and keep fresh, cold water at all times within reach of the animal. If constipation be present give warm water and glycerine enemas, and an occasional dose of castor oil if necessary. Should the bowels become too much relaxed with any tendency to inflammation, feed entirely on farinaceous food, arrowroot, farina or corn-starch with well boiled milk, as even beef-tea is somewhat of an irritant to the stomach and bowels. Carnrick's prepared food, which is lactated, is an excellent thing in these cases as it gives no work to the digestive apparatus, and is at once assimilated. Glover's Diarrhœa Cure should be given if necessity demands it. When symptoms of distemper first appear Glover's Distemper Cure should be given and persisted in for several days after all symptoms have disappeared to insure perfect recovery. An animal may have so far recovered that the owner considers it unnecessary to give any further medicine, the suspension of which will often result in a relapse, recovery from which is uncertain. In the treatment of distemper, one great object is to keep up the general strength, so in case of extreme debility a little whisky in milk or milk punches may be allowed.

The eyes should be bathed with warm water two or three times a day to keep them free of mucus, it will besides help to keep down inflammation. Should film form over the eyes or ulceration of the eyes or eyelids occur, Glover's Eye Lotion may be used with benefit. If at any time the accumulation of mucus in the air passages should be so great as to interfere with breathing, steaming the head will soften, detach and cause it to flow freely, thus giving relief, or in very urgent cases if the animal is comparatively strong, a mild emetic may be administered.

In the occurrnce of Fits, Glover's Cure for Fits should be given and a seton inserted at the back of the head. In Chorea, Arsenic or Bromide of Zinc will be useful. In Paralysis, Strychnine combined with general tonics should be given, and Glover's Liniment rubbed well in the entire length of the back, repeating night and morning until blister is produced. Electricity is here also strongly recommended.

In Pneumonia, Carbonate or Muriate of Ammonia, combined with expectorants should be given, also hot applications made externally, and alcoholic stimulants administered.

In Jaundice, give Glover's Liver Pills twice daily and apply mustard plaster over the region of the liver.

In recommending the use of Glover's Distemper Cure I do not claim that it is a panacea for all ills, but do maintain that it will cure any case of simple distemper when given in time.

LUKE WHITE'S KENNELS, Bridgeport, Conn.

MR. H. C. GLOVER:

Dear Sir:—Your Distemper Cure is the best thing I ever saw or heard of for dogs afflicted with that disease. I can't express myself too highly in its favor. It has saved several valuable puppies for me since the late New York dog show, among them a handsome terrier owned by Mr. Geo. J. Gould. This puppy was so bad at night that I had no hopes of finding him alive in the morning. I gave him the Distemper Cure merely to fulfill my last duty to him, but what was my surprise when I found him next morning gnawing on a bone which happened to be near his stall. He is now as well as

ever. I have had several such miraculous cures in my experience with it. It is a *positive* cure, when given in time, and will even be effectual when the patient seems on the very verge of death.
Yours, etc.,
LUKE W. WHITE.

Helena, Montana.

H. CLAY GLOVER, ESQ.:
Dear Sir:—Governor Crosby directs me to say he used your Distemper Cure with great success on his Irish setter bitch "Florence." The disease disappeared entirely in five days.
Very truly,
H. B. WILKINS, Jr.,
Private Secretary.

Meriden, Conn.

DR. H. CLAY GLOVER:
Dear Sir:—In using your Distemper Cure for distemper in dogs, I have never had a failure to cure, if taken when the dog could stand on his feet, and in several cases when they could not stand. Have had nearly one hundred cases.
Yours truly,　J. A. THOMAS.

Marion Junction, Ala.

DR. H. CLAY GLOVER :
Dear Sir :—Some time ago I sent for a bottle of your Distemper Cure and it is the best thing of the kind I ever saw. My dog was nearly dead, but is now all right.
Yours &c.,　C. CRENSHAW.

Hempstead, Long Island, N. Y.

H. CLAY GLOVER, V. S. :
Dear Sir :—We take pleasure in informing you we have used your Distemper Cure in our kennels with the most gratifying success. When taken in time we have not lost one in ten of the cases.
Truly Yours,
HEMPSTEAD FARM KENNELS.

Schenectady, N. Y.

Sir :—One week ago to-day my Irish setter dog was taken very sick with the distemper. I sent for your Distemper Cure and used part of one bottle, and to-day my dog is well as ever. I send you this for I think I owe it to you.
Yours truly,　GEO. A. ROSA,
228 Union Street.

MANGE

The term mange as applied to animals is identical with itch in the human race, in both of which parasitic life exists in the epidermis (skin) and is strictly a cutaneous disease.

The dog is afflicted with two varieties, namely, Sarcoptis Canis (Sarcoptic Mange), and Acarus Folliculorum (Follicular mange) which are frequently transmitted to other animals, and in several instances I have known it to be transmitted from the dog to humans, though it is quite unusual. Aside from these there are numerous skin diseases the dog is subject to that are too often confounded with true mange.

Eczema Rubrum, vulgarly called red mange, Erythema, Dematitis or surfeit, Psoriasis, Pityriasis, Erysipelas, etc., are all pronounced mange by the pretended knowing ones, whereas, they are not due to the presence of a parasite, but arise from other causes, viz., too much meat or corn-meal diet, with insufficient exercise, deranged condition of the digestive apparatus, worms, teething, sudden cooling of the body when heated, debilitating affections, injudicious use of mercurial preparations, local irritations, fleas, etc., and it is frequently necessary to make a microscopic examination to determine positively what the actual trouble is.

It is usually the case when a person has a sick animal, gratuitous advice is freely offered, which is almost invariably bad, and most all coachmen assume to be veterinary surgeons. To illustrate the latter, Mrs. Jones' little dog is afflicted with one of the many skin diseases. Mrs. Smith's coachman sees it, and at once pronounces it mange, saying that he will take it to his stable and cure it for a consideration. Mrs. Jones consents to being separated from her pet, with the assurance that it will only be for a short time. The coachman has some antiquated ideas of a mange wash which is persistently applied but without benefit. Other washes are then resorted to, with like result, and the coachman cannot understand why a local application will not cure a disease that requires constitutional treatment. The dog, after having been kept for an indefinite time is finally returned to its mis tress probably in worse condition than when she parted with it. Mrs. Jones now being actually frightened about her pet decides to consult some one qualified to treat him intelligently.

Sarcoptic Mange may be recognized by the following symptoms, viz., intense itching, small red points appearing on the skin, which quickly develop into, pustules, exuding a fluid which forms scabs. When from scratching or in other ways the scabs are removed, the hair will accompany them leaving the parts nude. The parasite usually first attacks the skin where most exposed from shortness or absence of hair, under the shoulders and thighs, about the hock joints, feet and eyes, are favorite places. It is not long confined to these localities, but rapidly spreads until the entire body is covered, unless checked by some application that will effectually destroy the parasites.

Follicular Mange though not causing the same amount of itching, is accompanied by a fetid body smell, the pustules sometimes giving out pus. The hair will be left standing firmly in places, while other parts may never again be as full in coat, owing to the hair follicles being destroyed by the parasites. Though this form of mange is not so annoying to the animal as the first-named variety, it does not yield as readily to treatment as Sarcoptic Mange, owing to the parasite being more deeply seated in the former. For the same reason it is not so easily transmitted.

Treatment.— Many preparations are used in the treatment of mange into which enter largely different forms of mercury, such as corrosive sublimate, red or white precipitate, of the ordinary mercurial ointment. The great objections to their use are, that they are rapidly absorbed and are productive of a form of eczema, termed Eczema Hydrargynia, or may cause salivation, besides rendering the animal particularly susceptible to colds or rheumatism. Again, it is necessary to keep the animal muzzled during their use to prevent his licking the poison, and a muzzle to some dogs is simply torture. Carbolic acid has also been recommended, but if used sufficiently strong to kill the parasites, will destroy the hair follicles. It is therefore desirable that something should be used that is harmless and at the same time effective. Glover's Mange Cure is a positive remedy for any and all cases of mange, effectually destroying the parasites, and contains no poison of any nature. It is so perfectly harmless that it might be given internally without any bad results. It would merely purge the bowels and have a beneficial effect on the blood.

It should be thoroughly well applied over the entire body, rubbing it well into the skin, and allowing it to remain on. Should a second application be necessary, it may be made three days later. Usually one or two applications are sufficient to effect a radical cure. Any case of skin trouble that it fails to effectually cure, may positively be determined as not a true mange. And although it will heal all such troubles arising from causes heretofore mentioned, the animal may continue to break out, in which case Glover's Blood Purifier should be given internally. If the trouble can be traced to impaired digestion or impoverished blood, Glover's Tonic will be of great benefit, together with change of diet, which in these cases, should consist entirely of well boiled meat.

For inflammatory conditions of the blood Fowler's Solution of Arsenic has been largely recommended, but necessitates being given a long time to derive a little effect, besides causing irritation of the stomach. I believe I am safe in saying that more actual alterative effect may be had from giving Glover's Blood Purifier three days than from giving Fowler's Solution three weeks.

As a kennel will become infected in time from keeping a mangy animal in it, after applying the Mange Cure, the kennel should be thoroughly disinfected, otherwise, there is fear of his retaking the disease. The better plan is to remove the animal to new quarters.

OFFICE OF MENAGERIE, Central Park, N. Y.

MR. H. CLAY GLOVER:

Dear Sir.—I take pleasure in giving my endorsement to your Mange Cure, having used it on camels, llamas, cattle and African wart hogs with perfect success. Would recommend it as a speedy cure for skin diseases.

Respectfully yours,

W. A. CONKLIN, V. S., Director.

Dr. H. C. Glover.
Dear Sir.—I have had your Mange Cure used at the kennels and on my own dogs with marked success.
ROBERT C. CORNELL,
Sec. Westminster Kennel Club.

Cincinnati, Ohio.
H. Clay Glover, Esq.:
Dear Sir.—I have used your Mange Cure for several years and find it entirely satisfactory. I have not had a case of mange in my kennels that your remedy has failed to cure in a very short time. Have not been obliged to use any other remedy as yours has accomplished all that is claimed for it.
Yours truly, W. B. SHATTUC.

THE MAIZELAND KENNELS, Red Hook, N. Y.
H. Clay Glover, D. V. S.:
Dear Sir.—I take great pleasure in recommending your Mang. Cure. Have used it in my kennels for over three years and always with entire satisfaction. Have also found it an excellen' remedy in the stable for scratches. Yours truly,
LAWRENCE TIMPSON

Cincinnati, Ohio.
Dr. H. Clay Glover:
Dear Sir.—Your Mange Cure is the best thing for scratches in horses I have ever used. Have cured six cases with three bottles.
Respectfully yours,
HENRY PEETE,
Foreman of Moerlin Brewing Co's Stables.

Peachers Mills, Tenn.
Dr. H. Clay Glover:
Dear Sir.—I have used your Mange Cure in seven very stubborn cases; it has never failed, and is certain death to a flea.
Yours truly,
H. O. HAMBAUGH.

Charleston, S. C.
Dear Sir.—I take special pleasure in recommending Glover's Mange Cure for mange in any of its stages. After curing the disease it leaves the skin of the animal in an excellent condition. As a flea destroyer it has no superior in the market.
Very truly yours,
THOS. R. GIBBS, Farrier & Horse-Shoer.

Fort Gibson, I. T.

MR. H. CLAY GLOVER:

Dear Sir.—Your Mange Cure arrived, and I used it on three dogs, and they are now well. It is the only real quick cure I know of. Yours truly,

HARRY S. GUYON.

Macedon, N. Y.

DR. H. CLAY GLOVER:

Dear Sir.—Your Mange Cure is the best remedy for scratches in horses I have ever used. It is a sure cure.

LYMAN BICKFORD.

THE FEDERAL BANK OF CANADA, London, Ont.

H. CLAY GLOVER, ESQ.:

Your Imperial Mange Cure is the best I ever saw or used. I have had spaniels very bad with mange and your Cure completely restored them. In fact, in a month the hair was as long as it ever was. I recommend it to any one having dogs afflicted in this way.

T. A. STEPHEN.

New York.

H. CLAY GLOVER, ESQ.:

Dear Sir.—I feel it my duty to notify you of the entire cure of my boy through the use of your Mange Cure. My boy had been under the care of my family physician for some time, and treated by him for what he termed dry Eczema. As my boy was growing worse and rapidly losing his hair, I concluded to try your Mange Cure. In less than two weeks the cure was assured, and the hair rapidly growing in, though the doctor said he would never again have hair on the bald spots. I should be glad to have you use this letter as one of the means of bringing your Mange Cure to the notice of the public.

Thankfully yours,

JAMES L. JACKSON, JR., 329 E. 28th St.

Claremont, N. H.

H. CLAY GLOVER:

My Dear Sir.—I am pleased to inform you that your Imperial Mange Cure has been of great benefit to me in curing my dogs whenever they have been afflicted with any skin trouble. I always keep it by me. Wishing you the success with it that it deserves, I am very truly, WM. JARVIS.

WORMS.

Worms, without doubt, cause the death, in various ways, of more puppies, and are more to be guarded against, than other diseases, from the fact that they may be destroying life when their presence is not suspected, except to those who are quite familiar with the symptoms. In discussing the subject of these internal para-sites I will merely touch upon those with which dogs are most commonly affected. Foremost, is the round worm, which inhabits the stomach and small intestines. They are of about the diameter of vermicelli, of a waxy color, from three to six inches in length, and pointed at each extremity. They will sometimes pass with the feces or may be vomited up, though their presence may not be made known in either way.

Of all varieties the round worms are to be most feared, are more peculiar to puppies and young dogs than adults, though the latter are frequently troubled with them. They cause great irritation of the stomach and intestines, giving rise to fits, indigestion, obstinate diar-rhœa, and are often present in such quantities as to cause obstruction of the bowels.

The *Maw-Worm* is of a slightly pinkish color, from half an inch to one inch in length, is located in the rectum, and though not dangerous, causes much irritation and is the source of great annoyance. It will sometimes produce partial paralysis in puppies, the paralysis disappearing after the worms are expelled. This worm is spoken of by some authors as being a segment of the tape-worm, but I am of the opinion that it is a distinct variety, as I have frequently found it present when there was no evidence of the existence of tape-worm. They are passed adhering to the feces, and are often seen sticking to the hair about the anus.

Tape-Worm.—There are a number of varieties of tape-worm to which the dog is subject, but as they all affect the animal in a similar manner, I shall not enter into their classification, but advise the same treatment for all.

The tape-worm is formed in sections of from one-quarter to one-half inch in length, white, and about as large round as a coarse thread. Is the most difficult of all worms to thoroughly eradicate, as portions will pass away from time to time; but so long as the head remains it will continue to grow. It is therefore necessary to persist in the use of a vermifuge until the head has been passed and this can only be positively arrived at by a microscopic examination of the matter voided.

Symptoms.—Restlessness, disturbed slumber, cough, unpleasant breath, nausea, colic pains, irregularity of the bowels, persistent diarrhœa, mucus passed with or following an action of the bowels, caked nose, perverted appetite, the animal swallowing foreign substances, such as ashes, coal, straw, bits of wood, etc. Pallid, visible membranes, especially in puppies, and a bloated appearance of the abdomen while thin elsewhere, Harsh, staring condition of the coat, dragging the hind part on the ground in a sitting position, all indicate the existence of some variety of worms.

Treatment.—Among the old-fashioned remedies for worms are powdered glass, tin filings, turpentine and Areca nut, all of which are extremely irritating to the mucous membranes covering the stomach and intestines. The most dangerous of these is Areca nut, which I have known to kill so many dogs that I am greatly opposed to its use. If fresh ground I believe it will produce gastro-enteritis, if stale it is quite inert.

As little or no action is derived from the use of vermifuge when there is food in the stomach, an animal should be fasted for at least twelve hours before administering it, and not fed sooner than two hours after. The advantages that I claim for Glover's Vermifuge over all others are, that while being equally efficacious, it is perfectly harmless to use, that it does not irritate the alimentary tract, but allays any irritation having been caused by worms, and that it does not require to be followed by a purgative, as is the case with others. As nine-tenths of all puppies have worms when born, I have always made it a rule to give those of my breeding some of the Vermifuge as soon as weaned, or even before, if I considered the case urgent. My idea is to get rid of the worms before they have done damage.

THE HOLLYWOOD, Long Branch.

DR. H. CLAY GLOVER:

Dear Sir.—I consider your medicines fa... superior to all others that I have ever used. The Vermifuge you prepare is really wonderful in its mild yet thorough action. Have used it most extensively on very young puppies with the best results.

Yours truly,   FRED HOEY.

Charleston, S. C.

Two puppies of mine were badly troubled with worms. I used the Vermifuge manufactured by H. Clay Glover, which completely cured them, and this Tonic brought them up to health in a short time. These were the only two saved from a litter of seven, the rest dying of worms and other sickness in other hands.

J. ALWYN BALL.

Hadlyme, Conn.

DR. H. CLAY GLOVER:

After using your Vermifuge on my Irish setter puppies, the masses of worms that passed from them was something dreadful. I consider your Vermifuge a wonderful thing and no owner of dogs should be without it.   Yours truly,

NEWTON ROSELLE.

Charleston, S. C.

Dear Sir.—I take pleasure in certifying to the excellence of Glover's Dog Remedies. With the Vermifuge I cured a dog of mine which I considered a hopeless case.   G. E. DAVIS,

City Sheriff.

———

FITS.

The dog is perhaps more subject to fits, or more properly epilepsy, than any other of the domestic animals, owing to his high development of brain and nervous system. Young animals are much more frequently its subjects than adults, as it is generally associated with puppy troubles, though dogs of mature age are occasionally so afflicted.

No premonitory symptoms are evinced in epilepsy, except perhaps, a slight quivering of the muscles, for a few seconds before the animal falls upon its side, losing consciousness, the limbs working violently, eyes set and froth issuing from the mouth. This condition usually lasts from ten to twenty minutes, or may be prolonged indefinitely, one attack following another in rapid succession, the latter usually occurring in distemper, resulting in death if not stopped. Upon an ordinary fit subsiding, consciousness or only partial consciousness will return. If the former, the animal will lie quietly for some time seemingly exhausted, or a comatose condition may exist for some minutes. If only partially conscious after an attack, the animal will run off in any direction for a mile or two, and when recovered will be found in some dark, out of the way place. In other cases the first symptoms may be absent, the animal on being attacked rushing away wildly, yelping as if in pain, running against objects as if partially blind, and perhaps snapping viciously. Many dogs are destroyed when in this condition, particularly if on a public thoroughfare, as the cry mad dog is at once raised ; whereas, all the poor animal requires is a little medicine and attention to restore him to his normal condition.

Causes.—Nervous excitement, worms, indigestion, protracted constipation, over heating, violent exercise after feeding, injuries about the head, and irritation incident to getting the second teeth and in bitches having suckling puppies, her abilities being overtaxed. Parturient apoplexy is liable to occur and must not be mistaken for epilepsy.

———

Treatment.--To successfully treat fits it is necessary to ascertain and remove the cause. If from worms, and it is safe to say all puppies have them, Glover's Vermifuge should be administered. If from teething, as soon as the milk teeth are loose they should be removed, and the gums, if inflamed, lanced where the second teeth are endeavoring to force their way through. Bones should also be allowed to bite on.

If from indigestion or any derangement of the gastric juices, the diet should consist for a time entirely of well boiled meat chopped fine, Glover's Tonic given, and the drinking water made one-fifth lime-water.

If from constipation, administer at once an enema of warm water and glycerine, and give Glover's Liver Pills for two or three nights successively.

If from nervous excitement, remove to a dark quiet place, and follow these directions, which are applicable during an attack of epilepsy, from any cause, viz., apply ice or cold water to the head, keeping the body warm, and give Glover's Cure for Fits every hour until several doses have been given. If the following day or at any time, any unusual excitement is observed a dose of the Cure will prevent an attack.

Animals subject to epilepsy should never be allowed violent exercise immediately after feeding, but kept as quiet as possible for several hours. Feed no hot food, sweets or pastries, all of which tend to disorder the stomach, producing indigestion, which gives rise to fits.

Puppies or young dogs when first taken into the street or field are extremely liable to fits, as new sights and noises will excite the nervous system; it is therefore best to gradually accustom them to these experiences.

CANKER OF THE EAR, INTERNAL.

This disease consists of ulcerous sores forming on the inside of the ears, which, if neglected, will after eating through the cartilage attack the bone, producing abcesses in the head and total deafness. It is the cause of great pain and annoyance, and should be treated on first symptoms appearing, when it may be readily cured. Whereas, if allowed to run on indefinitely, as is frequently the case, it is very obstinate. I find it much more prevalen tin long eared dogs than those of the small eared varieties, doubtless due to the fact that a large ear, besides retaining more heat in the head than a small one, also helps to hide from a careless owner the accumulation of dirt that is certain to occur when the ears are not properly looked after and cleansed

Frequently associated with internal canker is external canker, an ulcerous sore forming on the edge of the ear, caused by constant shaking of the head, which gradually eats into the leather (or flap of the ear).

External canker may originate from the ears being torn or scratched with briars, and will then exist independent of internal canker, but when the former is observed the latter should always be suspected and the ears thoroughly examined to ascertain if there be any internal trouble.

Causes.—Exposure to cold, being a great deal in the water, injuries due to a blow or kick, neglecting to keep the ears clean are all assigned as causes productive of internal canker. They may help towards its development, but I believe the origin of the trouble is an inflammatory condition of the blood, which exhibits itself in the form of internal canker on slight provocation. The fact of its frequently being associated with skin diseases is further evidence of its origin in the blood. Too much flesh or corn meal feeding will produce an inflammatory condition of the blood. Let me here say that for years I have been opposed to the use of corn meal, it being so heating in its character. Any other cereal is preferable. A coarse grade of wheat flour or rice is particularly nice. A vitiated condition of the blood, rendered so by some debilitating affection, will cause a pustulous eruption of the skin and internal canker.

Symptoms.—A red and inflamed appearance of the ears which have a heated feeling to the touch. Violent shaking of the head, scratching at the butt of the ear, often accompanied by whining or cries of pain. Pressing the ear to the ground. Tenderness to manipulation. A dark brown discharge, sometimes blood and pus, having an unpleasant odor. If the ear is thoroughly cleansed, small bright red spots will be observed.

Treatment.—If the animal is in high condition a sharp purgative should be given. Jalap will answer as well as anything. Increase the amount of exercise and restrict the diet to well boiled vegetables, cabbage, turnips, carrots, potatoes, etc. The ears should be thoroughly cleansed at least once a day, using warm water, adding ten drops of carbolic acid to the quart. Castile soap and a fine sponge or syringe will be necessary to remove all the discharge from the inside of the ears. If the syringe is employed, gentleness in its use should be observed. As a local application, Glover's Canker Wash should be used night and morning, warming it slightly to prevent any shock to the ear which is now particularly sensitive. If the trouble does not yield to this treatment as rapidly as is desired, it would be well to give Glover's Blood Purifier internally, Old cases require persistent treatment. Should the trouble arise from impoverished condition of the blood, dress the ears as heretofore directed, feed liberally and give Glover's Tonic internally. In case of external canker, touch the sore every other day with tincture muriate of iron, and apply iodoform ointment two or three times a day. Remove the collar and oblige the animal to wear a thin muslin cap to prevent his shaking his ears.

RHEUMATISM.

Rheumatism is a disease of the blood due to the presence of lithic acid. It may be acute or chronic. Some authors attribute the existence of rheumatism entirely to exposure to cold and dampness. This I must contradict, for in the absence of lithic acid there would be no rheumatism, though I concede that damp kennels, lying upon the earth, going into water when heated, etc., all tend to its development, the latter ofter producing an acute attack. Changes in the weather also have their effect. The parts of the dog most usually affected are the shoulders, the animal then moving like a foundered horse. This is generally termed kennel rheumatism. I have had many cases where the trouble was located in the muscles of the back, and sometimes in the abdominal muscles. It rarely attacks the joints.

Treatment.—Place the animal in warm, dry

quarters, and move the bowels thoroughly, saline aperients being especially indicated in this trouble. Salicylic acid, Colchicum, Iodide of Potash, Rhus Tox and Guaiacum are the usual remedies employed in the treatment of rheumatic troubles, but I would recommend Glover's Blood Purifier on account of the prompt alterative effect it has on the blood and in changing the secretions. Lime water should also be added to the drinking water, and Nitrate of Potash given when fever exists. Give Glover's Liver Pills every few days to keep the liver and bowels active. As a local application, nothing can be better than Glover's Liniment, which should be rubbed briskly into the affected parts night and morning. Hot fomentations are also serviceable.

OPTHALMIA.

Opthalmia, when first appearing, is a simple inflammation, caused by some foreign matter lodging in the eyes, a blow or scratch, and is frequently present in distemper, skin diseases, or any constitutional derangement.

The eyes are congested, evincing engorgement of the blood vessels, and have a watery appearance, the animal winking and showing a strong dislike to light. If the inflammation is not subdued a whitish film will form over one or both eyes, as the case may be, followed by ulceration of the pupils. The ulcers at the start have the appearance of slight depressions After opening, a fungus growth will take place.

Treatment.—Remove the animal to a dark place, move the bowels thoroughly, and keep on low, unstimulating diet. Bathe the eyes with water as warm as the animal can stand it for fifteen minutes at a time, several times a day, and use Glover's Eye Lotion night and morning. Local bleeding and a seton inserted at the back of the head will also be beneficial.

FLEAS.

Fleas keep a dog so busily employed scratching and biting himself that he gets but little sleep or rest. Between fleas and scratching much irritation of the skin is produced which in time assumes an eczematous form.

Besides the annoyance, the coat is gnawed off or torn out by the nails, giving to what has been a beautifully coated animal, a ragged, unkempt and unthrifty appearance. Constant vigilance is the price of keeping dogs free of fleas in warm weather, particularly if a number are kennelled together. An animal may be entirely rid of them one day. and have quantities the next, as they do not confine their homes for propagation to the dog's coat, but will breed in bedding, carpets cr sand, or the animal may get them from coming in contact with other dogs or cats harboring the ever busy Pulex irritans (Flea). In consequence of the rapid increase of these pests in sand, the dogs of California are much troubled with them. I might add the human race as well.

Treatment —For the destruction of these external parasites, all mercurial preparations, though efficacious, should not be used for the reasons given in the treatment of mange. Carbolic soap, or a solution of carbolic acid, is recommended, but I am opposed to their use from the fact that anything containing carbolic acid is injurious to the skin and coat, drying up the natural oils, thus rendering them dry and harsh. I use carbolic acid on dogs only as an antiseptic in case of abscesses, ulcers, unhealthy sores, or after operating. Glover's Mange Cure is instant death to fleas and will at the same time allay all irritation caused by scratching, etc.

If applied once or twice a week and allowed to remain on, fleas will not approach an animal so treated. On house or pet dogs it may be applied and washed off immediately after, and not a flea will be left alive. For toy dogs and those with particularly delicate skins my Kennel Soap might be tried, as it contains all the medicinal properties of the mange cure, but necessarily considerably modified by the body of the soap, which is of the finest of cocoanut and olive oils, avoiding even the use of potash in its manufacture, as all alkalies are destructive to the coat, and common soaps are largely made up of them:

GLOVER'S
IMPERIAL
DOG REMEDIES.

Mange Cure is a harmless and positive remedy for all skin diseases on animals; is instant death to fleas and vermin, and improves the growth of hair. For SCRATCHES IN HORSES or BAD SORES of any kind, it is unequalled; strictly non-poisonous. Price, 50 cents a bottle.

Distemper Cure is a safe and reliable cure for Distemper; subdues the fever at once, regulates the stomach, keeping up the appetite and general strength. A splendid thing for fever arising from any cause. Price, $1.00 a bottle.

Vermifuge is a safe and sure destroyer of all kinds of Worms in dogs. Price, 50 cents a bottle.

Canker Wash for internal Canker of the Ear. Price, 50 cents a bottle.

Eye Lotion for removing Film or Ulcers from the eyes. Price, 50 cents a bottle.

Blood Purifier is a great Blood Alterative, very quick in its action. Price, 50 cents a bottle.

Diarrhœa Cure, for acute or chronic diarrhœa and all bowel complaints. Price, 50 cents a bottle.

Cure for Fits will stop Fits or Convulsions in a few minutes. Price, 50 cents a bottle.

Tonic for debility arising from Distemper or other causes. Price, 50 cents a bottle.

Liniment for Rheumatism, Sprains or Bruises. Price, 50 cents a bottle.

Liver Pills act directly upon the Liver and Secretions. Price, 50 cents a box.

Kennel and Stable Soap contains in a modified form all the medicinal properties of the Mange Cure, compounded with the finest Cocoanut and Olive oils, making a soap equal in quality to any toilet soap. It contains no potash or carbolic acid, both of which are injurious to the coat, burning up the natural oil and in time rendering the skin dry and the coat harsh. GLOVER'S KENNEL AND STABLE SOAP is especially recommended for keeping the skin and coat in a healthy condition and is particularly good for any humor, irritation or sores. It is largely used for skin or scalp troubles in human beings. Price, 25 cents a cake.

The remedies referred to in this work are sold by druggists and dealers in sportsmen's goods. Should they not have them on hand they will get them for you.

N. B.—These preparations do not represent the fallacious and exploded ideas of twenty years ago, but are evidence of the advancement that has been made in Veterinary Medicine ; receiving the highest award at the American Institute Fair, New York, 1888, after being carefully analyzed by expert chemists.

NOTICE.

ALL COMMUNICATIONS

Requiring Advice

MUST BE ACCOMPANIED BY A FEE OF $2.00
TO INSURE ATTENTION.

H. Clay Glover, D.V.S.

1203 BROADWAY,

New York.

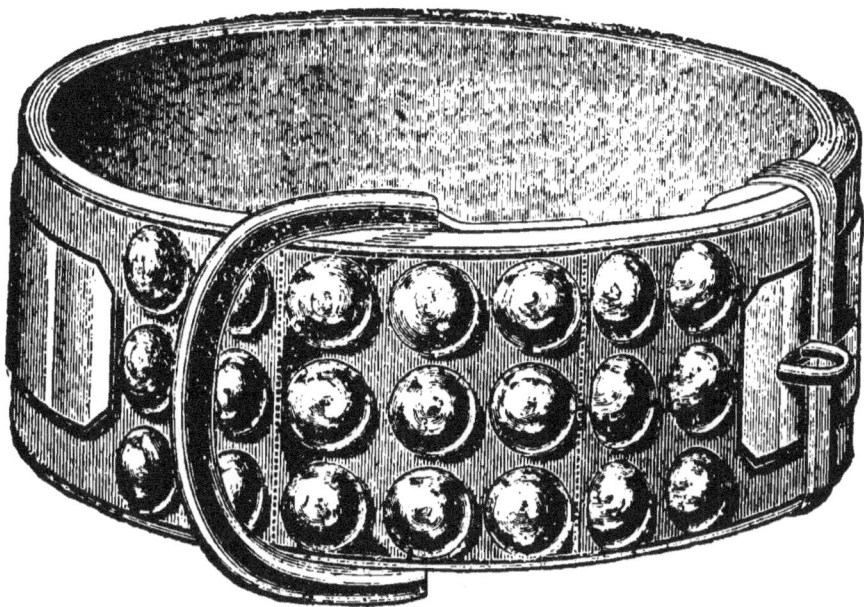

Glover's Album

A TREATISE ON

CANINE DISEASES

CONCISE AND PRACTICAL.

HANDSOMELY BOUND & ILLUSTRATED